**DATE DUE**

| | | | |
|---|---|---|---|
| | | | |
| | | | |
| | | | |
| | | | |
| | | | |
| | | | |
| | | | |
| | | | |
| | | | |
| | | | |
| | | | |
| | | | |
| | | | |
| | | | |
| | | | |
| | | | |

DEMCO 38-297

# BASEBALL LEGENDS

*Hank Aaron*
*Grover Cleveland Alexander*
*Ernie Banks*
*Johnny Bench*
*Yogi Berra*
*Roy Campanella*
*Roberto Clemente*
*Ty Cobb*
*Dizzy Dean*
*Joe DiMaggio*
*Bob Feller*
*Jimmie Foxx*
*Lou Gehrig*
*Bob Gibson*
*Rogers Hornsby*
*Reggie Jackson*
*Shoeless Joe Jackson*
*Walter Johnson*
*Sandy Koufax*
*Mickey Mantle*
*Christy Mathewson*
*Willie Mays*
*Stan Musial*
*Satchel Paige*
*Brooks Robinson*
*Frank Robinson*
*Jackie Robinson*
*Pete Rose*
*Babe Ruth*
*Nolan Ryan*
*Mike Schmidt*
*Tom Seaver*
*Duke Snider*
*Warren Spahn*
*Willie Stargell*
*Casey Stengel*
*Honus Wagner*
*Ted Williams*
*Carl Yastrzemski*
*Cy Young*

CHELSEA HOUSE PUBLISHERS

# ERNIE
# BANKS

*Peter C. Bjarkman*

*Introduction by*
**Jim Murray**

---

*Senior Consultant*
*Earl Weaver*

CHELSEA HOUSE PUBLISHERS
*New York • Philadelphia*

**CHELSEA HOUSE PUBLISHERS**

*Editorial Director:* Richard Rennert
*Executive Managing Editor:* Karyn Gullen Browne
*Copy Chief:* Robin James
*Picture Editor:* Adrian G. Allen
*Art Director:* Robert Mitchell
*Manufacturing Director:* Gerald Levine
*Production Coordinator:* Marie Claire Cebrián-Ume

**Baseball Legends**
*Senior Editor:* Philip Koslow

**Staff for ERNIE BANKS**
*Editorial Assistant:* Kelsey Goss
*Designer:* M. Cambraia Magalhães
*Picture Researcher:* Alan Gottlieb
*Cover Illustration:* Daniel O'Leary

First Printing

1 3 5 7 9 8 6 4 2

**Library of Congress Cataloging-in-Publication Data**

Bjarkman, Peter C.
Ernie Banks / Peter C. Bjarkman; introduction by Jim Murray;
senior consultant, Earl Weaver.
    p.   cm. —(Baseball legends)
Includes bibliographical references and index.
Summary:  A biography of the baseball player who hit over 500
home runs in his nineteen seasons with the Chicago Cubs.
ISBN 0-7910-1167-4.
ISBN 0-7910-1201-8 (pbk.)
1. Banks, Ernie, 1931– —Juvenile literature.  2. Baseball
players—United States—Biography—Juvenile literature.
3. Chicago Cubs (Baseball team)—History—Juvenile
literature.  [1. Banks, Ernie, 1931– .  2. Baseball players.
3. Afro-Americans—Biography.]  I. Title.  II. Series.
GV865.B26B53  1992                               91-28901
796.357'092—dc20                                 CIP
[B]                                              AC

921
Ban

# CONTENTS

163644

# WHAT MAKES A STAR

*Jim Murray*

No one has ever been able to explain to me the mysterious alchemy that makes one man a .350 hitter and another player, more or less identical in physical makeup, hard put to hit .200. You look at an Al Kaline, who played with the Detroit Tigers from 1953 to 1974. He was pale, stringy, almost poetic-looking. He always seemed to be struggling against a bad case of mononucleosis. But with a bat in his hands, he was King Kong. During his career, he hit 399 home runs, rapped out 3,007 hits, and compiled a .297 batting average.

Form isn't the reason. The first time anybody saw Roberto Clemente step into the batter's box for the Pittsburgh Pirates, the best guess was that Clemente would be back in Double A ball in a week. He had one foot in the bucket and held his bat at an awkward angle—he looked as though he couldn't hit an outside pitch. A lot of other ballplayers may have had a better-looking stance. Yet they never led the National League in hitting in four different years, the way Clemente did.

Not every ballplayer is born with the ability to hit a curveball. Nor is exceptional hand-eye coordination the key to heavy hitting. Big-league locker rooms are filled with players who have all the attributes, save one: discipline. Every baseball man can tell you a story about a pitcher who throws a ball faster than anyone has ever seen but who has no control on or *off* the field.

The Hall of Fame is full of people who transformed themselves into great ballplayers by working at the sport, by studying the game, and making sacrifices. They're overachievers—and winners. If you want to find them, just watch the World Series. Or simply read about New York Yankee great Lou Gehrig; Ted Williams, "the Splendid Splinter" of the Boston Red Sox; or the Dodgers' strikeout king Sandy Koufax.

A pitcher *should* be able to win a lot of ballgames with a 98-miles-per-hour fastball. But what about the pitcher who wins 20 games a year with a fastball so slow that you can catch it with your teeth? Bob Feller of the Cleveland Indians got into the Hall of Fame with a blazing fastball that glowed in the dark. National League star Grover Cleveland Alexander got there with a pitch that took considerably longer to reach the plate; but when it did arrive, the pitch was exactly where Alexander wanted it to be—and the last place the batter expected it to be.

There are probably more players with exceptional ability who didn't make it to the major leagues than there are who did. A number of great hitters, bored with fielding practice, had to be dropped from their team because their home-run production didn't make up for their lapses in the field. And then there are players like Brooks Robinson of the Baltimore Orioles, who made himself into a human vacuum cleaner at third base because he knew that working hard to become an expert fielder would win him a job in the big leagues.

A star is not something that flashes through the sky. That's a comet. Or a meteor. A star is something you can steer ships by. It stays in place and gives off a steady glow; it is fixed, permanent. A star works at being a star.

And that's how you tell a star in baseball. He shows up night after night and takes pride in how brightly he shines. He's Willie Mays running so hard his hat keeps falling off; Ty Cobb sliding to stretch a single into a double; Lou Gehrig, after being fooled in his first two at-bats, belting the next pitch off the light tower because he's taken the time to study the pitcher. Stars never take themselves for granted. That's why they're stars.

# "I WAS PETRIFIED!"

*Ernie Banks poses on the dugout steps at Wrigley Field in August 1955. Breaking in with the Cubs in 1953, Banks quickly established himself as the hardest-hitting shortstop in memory. His Hall of Fame career spanned 19 seasons.*

On the morning of September 14, 1953, a slender 21-year-old black man walked through the players' entrance of historic Wrigley Field, the home of the Chicago Cubs. Guided by Roy "Hard Rock" Johnson, a Chicago coach, the young man climbed the stairs to the second level and crossed a concrete ramp that led to the Cubs clubhouse. It was an exciting but tension-filled moment for the youthful Texan, who had been playing ball for the Kansas City Monarchs in the Negro American League. He knew that established big leaguers were often hostile to rookies, who were hoping to take someone's job away. In addition, he was well aware that the Cubs had never before had a black player on their roster, and he had no idea how the white players would respond to him. As he later recalled in his autobiography, *Mr. Cub,* "I was where I had always hoped to be—and I was petrified!"

When Johnson ushered the newcomer through the door, only three players were in the locker room. The young man's nervousness increased when he realized that one of the players was Hank Sauer, a burly veteran who had tied for the league lead in home runs the previous year, winning the National League's Most

Valuable Player Award. The other two players were infielders Randy Jackson and Bill Serena, both seasoned major leaguers who had been Chicago regulars for several years.

"This is Ernie Banks," Johnson told the trio of veterans. "He's going to be with us for the rest of the season."

Banks was deeply relieved when the three players cordially shook his hand. Sauer was especially gracious, telling the rookie that he was pleased to meet him and hoped he would do good things for the ballclub. Banks could not have been more pleased when he learned that he was being given the locker right next to Sauer's. When he had his uniform on and was following Johnson down to the field, the two men crossed paths with outfielder Ralph Kiner, who had been traded to the Cubs from the Pittsburgh Pirates earlier in the season. Kiner was one of baseball's true superstars, a powerful slugger who had been the National League's home run king for seven straight years (he had tied with Sauer in 1952), hitting a high of 54 round-trippers in 1949. Kiner was every bit as gracious as Sauer had been. "What a great reception," Banks recalled, "meeting two home run hitters like Hank Sauer and Ralph Kiner and having both of them say they were glad to meet me, me, Mr. Nobody from Dallas."

Banks loosened up and then took fielding practice. After the regulars had finished batting practice, he was finally summoned to the batting cage along with the other reserves. He had not been sure-handed while taking ground balls at shortstop, and as he prepared to hit, he said to himself, If you don't hit better than you fielded, they'll be sending you back to the Monarchs tomorrow night.

As he approached the batting cage, Banks noticed one of Kiner's bats lying on the ground. As a rookie, he had no bats of his own yet, and he called over to Kiner, asking permission to use the slugger's lumber. Kiner said he had no objection but wondered if his bat was the right weight and length for Banks. When Kiner, who was used to getting custom-made bats shipped to him free of charge, asked what model the rookie had been using, Banks hardly knew what to say. "I had to tell him that where I came from we were happy to have bats, period."

When Banks walked into the batting cage and took his stance at the plate, Hard Rock Johnson wound up and fired a batting practice pitch from the mound. Banks stepped into the delivery and uncoiled his short, quick swing. The ball jumped off his bat and soared on a high arc toward left field, coming down at last in the still-empty bleachers behind the picturesque ivy-covered outfield wall.

"There was a sort of silence," Banks recalled, "until Ralph Kiner yelled, 'Hey Banks, you can use all my bats if you promise to keep on hitting like that!'"

Banks did keep on hitting like that, and before long other players were borrowing *his* bats. His 19 years in a Cubs uniform were remarkable not only for the 512 home runs he smashed but even more so for the devotion he earned from Cubs fans and finally from the entire city of Chicago. For the down-to-earth Chicagoans, Banks was both an ideal athlete and an ideal human being: one who greeted each day with a smile, never sulked or made excuses, put his heart and soul into his work, cherished his friends and family, and never forgot where he came from.

*Ralph Kiner, who led the National League in home runs for seven straight seasons while playing for the Pittsburgh Pirates, came to the Cubs in a trade during the 1953 season. When Banks joined the team late in the year, Kiner was one of the established stars who made him feel welcome.*

# 2

# CHILD OF
# THE DEPRESSION

**E**rnest Banks was born on January 31, 1931, in Dallas, Texas. As it turned out, that year of deprivation for the U.S. economy was to produce a bumper crop of Hall of Fame sluggers who hit 500 or more home runs in the major leagues. Following Banks, Willie Mays was born on May 6, 1931, in Westfield, Alabama; Eddie Mathews came into the world on October 13, in Texarkana, Texas; and Mickey Mantle was born a week later, on October 20, in Spavinaw, Oklahoma.

Like many future big leaguers, Ernie had a father who was in love with the game of baseball. Eddie Banks had been a successful catcher for the Dallas Black Giants and Houston Buffalos in the black semipro leagues that thrived at a time when black athletes were not permitted to play in the majors. And Eddie Banks, like so many other fathers, had dreams of athletic glory for his firstborn son.

But in the early years of his life, baseball was far removed from the world of Ernie Banks. The youngster was born into a poor working-class Dallas family, in the depths of the economic depression that had gripped the United States since 1929. He was the second of the 12 children born to Eddie and Essie Banks. The Bankses

*A view of downtown Dallas, Texas, around 1930. When Ernie Banks was born in the city the following year, the United States was in the grip of the Great Depression. Though the Bankses had little money, they were a close-knit and loving family.*

were hardworking people who labored from sunup until sundown—and often beyond—to provide food, clothing, and a warm, if rustic, home for their ever-expanding family. For several years Eddie Banks labored at the backbreaking work of cotton picking; later he was a construction worker for the Works Progress Administration (WPA), a government program set up to provide jobs for the disadvantaged. Often holding down more than one job at a time, Eddie Banks also worked as a warehouse loader and as a stock clerk in a grocery store. Essie Banks, in addition to all her household duties, worked long hours as a cleaning lady in a local bank. "Despite their hardships," their oldest son later recalled, "my parents always stressed togetherness within the family. They taught us love and the importance of right thinking."

In later years, everyone in the Banks family remembered young Ernie as a model child. He faithfully attended Sunday school and church services, and though he was never a dedicated student, he would often read alone in his room into the late hours of evening. Ernie also tried his hand at a variety of jobs, such as picking cotton, shining shoes, and carrying out garbage cans from a local hotel.

During his high school years, Ernie played some YMCA league softball during the summer months and showed great skill at the game. He had a natural batting stroke and gracefully roamed the infield from the shortstop position, which he enjoyed playing most. But his school, Booker T. Washington High School, did not field a baseball team when he was there, so he lacked the incentive to develop a true attachment to the game.

Football and basketball loomed larger than baseball in young Ernie's life during high school, but even here he did not have an easy road to

*Banks lights a cigar for his father, Eddie, before a Cubs game in June 1958. The elder Banks, a catcher in the black semipro leagues, had been denied a major league career by baseball's color line. Though working long hours to feed his 12 children, he took time to nurture their athletic talents.*

follow. In fact, it took a good deal of outside intervention just to get him playing in the official school leagues. As a 5-foot-6, 150-pound high school sophomore, Ernie was simply too shy and lacking in self-confidence to try out for any of the school's athletic teams. Bill Blair, one of the Banks's neighbors, provided the much-needed nudge.

One day, while Ernie and Blair watched the high school's spring football practice from the sidelines, Blair asked Ernie why he was not out there himself. Ernie could only offer that he was far too small to play, at which point Blair called out to his friend Ray Hollie, the coach of the squad. "Ray, this boy here is a cinch to make your team." When the coach suddenly walked over and ordered the startled youngster to report to the gym for a uniform, Ernie was simply too shocked to offer any arguments. Once on the field, Ernie ran circles around the defense, and the delighted coach was not about to let him get away.

Ernie became a genuine star on the football field. He caught 22 touchdown passes during his final two high school seasons and captained the team. He played basketball with equal brilliance, averaging nearly 15 points a game in an era when a whole team rarely scored more than 30 or 40. In the sport of track and field, where he also performed for Washington High, he high-jumped over 6 feet, long-jumped better than 19 feet, and ran the quarter mile in the excellent time of 51 seconds.

In the summer of 1948, another push from Bill Blair got Ernie into organized baseball. At the time, the youngster was playing around the Dallas area with a ragged semipro softball team. Ernie was practicing on a sandlot with a few of his teammates when Blair showed up with a friend named Jim Carter. The two men were involved with a semipro black baseball club often called the Detroit Colts, even though they actually played their home games in Amarillo, 360 miles from Dallas. Blair and Carter had one thing in mind, and that was signing up Ernie for the Colts.

Blair and Carter sold Ernie on the idea and accompanied him home for a pep talk with his parents. They pointed out to Eddie and Essie Banks that Ernie had a wonderful opportunity to see something of the world and also make some spare pocket change in the bargain.

Eddie Banks was all for the idea, but Ernie's mother required a much harder sell. She peppered the two small-town baseball executives with questions about her son's well-being and safety. Because Blair and his wife would travel with the team—Blair was the manager on the road—it seemed a safe enough proposition even to a skeptical mother. Once she had a firm promise that Ernie would be back home that fall in plenty of time to finish his final year of high school, Essie Banks gave her permission.

Soon Ernie was off on his first baseball tour. "It was my first trip away from Dallas," he later recalled, "and I was goggle-eyed watching the scenery as we rolled west through little towns." The team would pile up miles and miles between June and late August playing daily games in small towns throughout West Texas, New

Mexico, Oklahoma, Kansas, and Nebraska. Ernie later compared his sense of discovery and wonder to the emotions that astronauts experienced during space travel.

Ernie also never forgot the first home run of his barnstorming baseball career. He hit the round-tripper in his very first home game with the Colts. The big blast came on his third trip to the plate, and he later recalled that the wind was blowing out strongly toward left field. When the ball cleared the wooden fence, Ernie found himself bounding around the bases, while the cheers of the handful of fans gathered on that June Texas night sounded in his ears like the roar of thousands.

But when Ernie reached the dugout, he was shocked to find Blair shouting at him to get his hat off and get himself up into the stands while the excited fans were still on their feet. The youngster had not heard about the customary practice of the local black fans, who would drop coins into the hats of their heroes after each and every home team circuit blast.

The homer was the first of many more to come. And a few years down the road, Ernie would be hitting them for a lot more money than the change he collected in his cap that night in Amarillo.

# 3 BARNSTORMING

Fans of the barnstorming black baseball leagues discovered Ernie Banks long before the world of white baseball knew anything of his budding talents. While playing for the Detroit Colts, Banks had appeared in several exhibition games against the touring Kansas City Monarchs of the Negro American League. The Monarchs were the dominant team in black baseball at the time, and they were always mining the small towns and amateur leagues for new talent.

Soon there was a second meeting of anxious black baseball scouts with Eddie and Essie Banks to discuss their son's future. The Bankses were pleased with Ernie's happy experience during his first summer of baseball touring and saw no reason to hold him back. Besides, the $300 a month that the Kansas City club was offering seemed like a fortune to the hardworking couple who had fought their way through the Great Depression.

After his high school graduation in the summer of 1950, Ernie joined the famed Monarchs in Kansas City for the start of a new baseball season. The team's tours would range from major cities, such as Chicago, to smaller communities, such as Biloxi, Mississippi. Some of

*Banks in the uniform of the Kansas City Monarchs during the early 1950s. Playing for the Monarchs, the best team in the Negro leagues, gave Banks a chance to tour the United States and brought him to the attention of big league scouts.*

the games would even be played in such prestigious big league stadiums as Chicago's Comiskey Park and New York's Yankee Stadium.

By the time Banks joined the Monarchs for the 1950 season, the exodus of talented black players to the major leagues had already begun. A decade earlier the Negro leagues boasted star players who regularly defeated major leaguers in off-season barnstorming exhibitions. They featured such pitching greats as Satchel Paige, Smokey Joe Williams, and Bullet Joe Rogan, along with such awesome sluggers as Josh Gibson, Oscar Charleston, and Williard "Home Run" Brown. But Jackie Robinson had finally broken baseball's color line when he took the field for the Brooklyn Dodgers in 1947, and his brilliant play convinced the other big league teams to follow the Dodgers' lead. Now that black fans could see stars like Robinson, the Cleveland Indians' Larry Doby, and the New York Giants' Monte Irvin in big league uniforms, the Negro leagues were no longer the attraction that they had once been in the black community. One by one the black teams were disbanding, and the league was a shadow of its earlier self. For Ernie Banks, however, this was the first taste of big-time professional baseball, and it was a thrilling experience.

Years later, Banks vividly remembered his first pro game for the Monarchs against the Indianapolis Clowns in Kansas City's old Blues Stadium. "I had never seen a park as big as that one, much less played in one," he recalled. "All I wanted to do was look around and get the feel of everything, the well-manicured green grass, the big advertising signs on the outfield fences, the huge dugouts complete with water fountains, and the massive grandstands."

This looked like the big time to Banks, but few of today's baseball fans (or players) can imagine what barnstorming with the black teams of the 1940s and 1950s was like. Between games, teams traveled all night in rickety old buses that served as sleeping quarters as well as transportation. Players were lucky to get two or three dollars a day for meals, and they wore the same unlaundered uniform for months on end. Many games had but one umpire, the ballpark lights were often dim, and the schedule often stretched to more than 200 games a year. But the baseball atmosphere was always magical, and the crowds of both black and white rooters were usually large and enthusiastic.

During Banks's final month with the touring Monarchs, Buster Hayward, the player-manager of the Indianapolis Clowns, asked the youngster to telephone him as soon as the season was over. When Banks made the call, Hayward had surprising and exciting news. Jackie Robinson was organizing a touring all-star team to barnstorm throughout the South with the Indianapolis Clowns, directly after the big league World Series, and Banks was being invited to join the tour.

*The Pittsburgh Crawfords, 1935 champions of the Negro National League. Continually on the road, Negro leaguers had a much harder life than their white counterparts. They received little money for expenses and often had to sleep in the buses that carried them from city to city.*

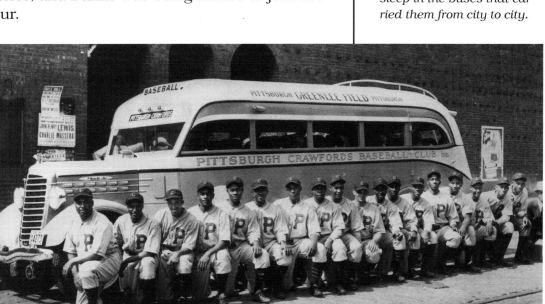

Banks soon found himself in Jacksonville, Florida, overwhelmed by the opportunity to play ball alongside such legends as Jackie Robinson, Roy Campanella, Don Newcombe, and other big leaguers. He had been told that he would do double duty at shortstop, playing one day for Robinson's team and the next for the Indianapolis ballclub.

Banks's biggest thrill of the year was his first face-to-face meeting with the legendary Robinson. It happened before a game in Meridian, Mississippi. Banks was standing quietly alongside the batting cage when Robinson approached. "I've been watching you, young man," Robinson said. "You can really pull that inside pitch. You hit very well." Never before had Banks received such a compliment from such a respected source. For days afterward, he felt that his feet were barely touching the ground. And during the brief tour, Robinson followed up with more encouragement and practical advice. The Brooklyn star gave Banks pointers on fielding and suggested he work on perfecting his release while making the double play.

Before Banks could even think of fulfilling his baseball dreams, he received notice to report for military service. In the spring of 1951, he was inducted into the U.S. Army and assigned to a battalion made up mostly of young black recruits from Texas, Alabama, and Mississippi. A few months later, Banks and his unit shipped out for a tour of duty in Germany.

U.S. troops were fighting in Korea in 1951, but fortunately for Banks Europe was at peace. Before long, he was chosen to play on his battalion's baseball team, which competed in a six-team European military league. Banks's talented squad stood second in the standings during the season's first half, with Banks playing shortstop. But injuries would eventually eliminate them from the league race.

Racial segregation in the armed forces had come to an end in 1948. Blacks and whites were now officially on an equal footing, and black soldiers had more opportunities for promotion. At the end of the baseball season, Banks was named company athletic director. Among his duties was the organization of company teams in football, basketball, and boxing.

By the time he was discharged from the military in March 1953, Banks was anxious to get back to full-time baseball with the Kansas City Monarchs. And the Monarchs, now falling increasingly on hard times, were eager to have him back in the lineup. While Banks was in the service, both the Cleveland Indians and the Brooklyn Dodgers had contacted him, inviting him for tryouts when he returned. But Banks was only interested in being reunited with his old teammates and with Monarchs manager Buck O'Neil.

Nevertheless, by the end of the 1953 season, Banks found himself in Wrigley Field, playing major league baseball for the Chicago Cubs. There are conflicting stories about how this came to pass. One account suggests that Bill Veeck—then the owner of the American League's St. Louis Browns and one of baseball's most inventive and colorful executives—tried to buy Banks's contract from Monarchs owner Tom Baird, who was strapped for cash. But the deal fell through because Veeck himself was low on funds and could not meet Baird's asking price. Veeck then requested that Baird at least sell the

Banks (front row, second from right) poses with other black major leaguers during a barnstorming tour in 1955. Banks had joined his first barnstorming tour when still in the Negro leagues, and the praise of stars such as Jackie Robinson had inspired him to shoot for the big time.

budding star to a team in the National League so that he would never compete against the Browns. Veeck also wanted to keep Banks away from the Browns' crosstown rivals, the St. Louis Cardinals, so he suggested contacting the Chicago Cubs.

Whatever the extent of Veeck's involvement, there is no question that the Cubs were already scouting Banks by the summer of 1953. The team had previously tabbed Gene Baker, a promising shortstop playing in the Pacific Coast League, as the first black player who would wear a Cubs uniform. But Ernie Banks was too big a talent to pass up.

In early September, Baird went to Chicago for a secret meeting with Cubs general manager Wid Matthews. When Matthews inquired what it would cost the Cubs to purchase both Banks and pitching prospect Bill Dickey in a package deal, Baird demanded $15,000 for his shortstop and $5,000 more for the promising hurler. The deal was quickly agreed on, and when the Monarchs' season came to an end a week later, Banks was on his way to Chicago. Bill Dickey, despite having the same name as the great New York Yankees catcher of the 1930s and 1940s, would never appear in a single big league game. But the Cubs management was already certain that they had got their money's worth, and more.

# 4

# "LET'S PLAY TWO!"

**E**rnie Banks is remembered by fans nearly as much for his catchy sayings as he is for his booming bat and talented glove. "This is the year of the little bear," he would tell reporters at the beginning of each new season and then invent a catchphrase for the campaign. "The Cubbies thrive in sixty-five." "Things look great in sixty-eight." "The Cubbies will shine in sixty-nine." But his most famous line of all is the one that summed up Banks's love for daily ballgames in front of the friendly hometown fans and under the blue skies at sun-drenched Wrigley Field. "It's a beautiful day for baseball! Let's play two today!"

Banks was immediately thrust into the spotlight as the first black player to suit up for the Cubs, even though he was far from being the first in the major leagues. He had already been preceded by Jackie Robinson, Roy Campanella, Don Newcombe, and Dan Bankhead in Brooklyn; Larry Doby, Luke Easter, and Satchel Paige with the Cleveland Indians; Willie Mays, Hank Thompson, and Monte Irvin of the New York Giants; Minnie Minoso with the crosstown White Sox; and 1950 N.L. Rookie of the Year Sam Jethroe with the Boston Braves. By the time Banks stepped onto the playing field at

*Banks and Milwaukee Braves star Hank Aaron look toward the fences at Wrigley Field on September 21, 1957. When this photo was taken, the former Negro league stars were dueling for the National League home run crown: Banks was leading with 42 homers, and Aaron was only 1 behind.*

Wrigley in 1953, blacks were no longer taunted by fans and opposing players as they had been during Robinson's and Doby's early seasons.

But Banks was still a pioneer. He was, for one thing, one of the last two stars from the Negro leagues to step into major league play. The other was his longtime rival Hank Aaron, who made his debut the following year with the Braves, who had moved to Milwaukee. Together with Willie Mays, Banks and Aaron created a revolution in the art of long-ball hitting.

Before the heyday of the young black stars, home run hitters had largely been big, plodding

*Orestes "Minnie" Minoso of the Chicago White Sox was one of several black stars already in the major leagues when Banks arrived in 1953. With baseball's color line only a memory, Banks and second baseman Gene Baker encountered no problems as the first African Americans to play for the Cubs.*

types who wielded big slabs of lumber. Ralph Kiner, Hank Sauer, and the Cardinals' Johnny Mize were recent sluggers who fit this mold. More often than not, the home run hitters were average or below-average fielders whose flaws with the glove were overlooked because they could hit the long ball. Banks, Aaron, and Mays, in addition to being top-notch fielders and swift baserunners, also brought a new style of slugging into the game. Lean and muscular in build, they were free swingers who used exceptional arm speed and wrist action to snap the ball into orbit.

Banks was actually the original master of the new hitting style. His power derived mainly from his forearms. "He may look thin," Philadelphia Phillies pitching great Robin Roberts once observed, "but from the elbows down he's got the incredible muscles of a 230-pounder!" In addition to his strength, Banks had perfected a compact, lightning-quick batting stroke. Cubs catcher Clyde McCullough noted, "He swings a lot like Joe Louis used to throw a punch—short and sweet." During his early years, Banks's weapon of choice was a 31-ounce bat that he whipped into the ball in much the same manner as a golfer. Soon other hitters were adopting lighter bats and imitating Banks's swing.

Before Banks, baseball had never seen such a combination of finesse and power at the shortstop position. Traditionally, shortstops are light hitters. The position requires so much mental and physical energy that teams do not expect their shortstop to punish the ball; they are willing to sacrifice offense for a solid job in the field. Thus, for all Banks's power, he would not have helped his team if he had been a mediocre fielder. Admittedly, his throwing arm was not exceptional by big league standards, but he covered the left side of the infield with a grace and agility few could match. In 1954, he turned 105 double plays, a total never bettered; in 1959, he led the league with a .985 fielding average, setting a record that stood for 12 years.

Banks established his credentials as a slugger in 1954, his first full season, when he belted 19 homers and drove in 79 runs. The following year, he bashed National League pitching for the lofty totals of 44 homers and 117 runs batted in, while compiling a .295 batting average. In many years before and since, 44 home runs would have led the league. But in 1955, Mays clouted 51 round-trippers for the Giants, and Cincinnati muscleman Ted Kluszewski clubbed 47. Banks had to settle for third place in the home run derby, still a great distinction for a shortstop, and his RBI total was the league's fourth best. During that same summer the new Chicago hitting phenom banged out five grand slams, eclipsing a long-standing record.

However, big league baseball was not going to be quite so easy for Banks, any more than it is for any young performer. While Banks seemed to own the league in 1955, the talented and experienced big league hurlers were comparing notes. Before long, they began to uncover and exploit his weaknesses.

When the 1956 campaign got underway, Banks found that many pitchers were pitching him outside, giving him nothing he could reach easily with his dangerous bat and taking advantage of his tendency to chase bad balls. Then, when they had him leaning forward to protect the outer half of the plate, they would come back

inside with pitches so tight that even Banks's quick bat could not get around on them.

Banks was soon struggling. He spent the year desperately trying to adjust at the plate. By the end of the season, he succeeded in raising his batting average to .297. But his power numbers fell off dramatically: he ended 1956 with 28 home runs and 85 RBIs. Any other shortstop in the league would have been thrilled with those totals. Brooklyn's Pee Wee Reese, for example, a future Hall of Famer, batted .257 in 1956, with 9

*Banks prepares to lace into a pitch at Cincinnati's Crosley Field in 1958. Along with Hank Aaron and Willie Mays, Banks revolutionized the art of long-ball hitting by using a lighter bat and drawing power from the whiplike action of his wrists and forearms.*

home runs and 46 RBIs. But Banks had already set such a high standard for himself that he could only regard 1956 as a bitter disappointment.

And while he struggled at the plate in 1956, Banks soon found himself struggling in the field as well. His arm tired as the season progressed, and this caused him to move in at shortstop. The move helped his throwing, but quite a few balls got past him for base hits. The Cubs soon decided that a change might be needed. In 1957, Banks started at third base for 58 games. Always a team player, he attempted valiantly to adjust. But the more stationary position was just not natural to him, and his weak arm became even more of a drawback when he tried to make the long throw across the diamond. The switch to third did boost Banks's run production—he finished the 1957 season with 43 homers and 102 RBIs—but he knew that he was not helping the team in the field. And the Cubs, who finished last in 1956 and next-to-last in 1957, needed all the help they could get.

Some nay-sayers were soon arguing that Banks would never become the all-around player the Cubs expected him to be. But Banks himself never doubted. He took the field every day with enthusiasm and the determination to work hard. This was the only approach he knew.

Some of Banks's problems stemmed from a sore knee, the result of an injury he had first suffered during his military years. As the knee grew stronger during the 1957–58 off-season, Banks's confidence slowly returned also. When he opened the 1958 season back at shortstop, he was completely relaxed. The new strength in his knee improved his range and also helped his throwing. He moved farther back on the infield again and began to patrol his position as skillfully as he had during his seasons with the Kansas City Monarchs. Playing all 154 games, he compiled a record number of fielding chances.

While starring in the field, Banks was also terrorizing the National League's pitchers. His average jumped up to .313, and he led the league in home runs (47), RBIs (129), total bases (379), and slugging average (.614). Banks's dominance made him a shoo-in for the N.L. Most Valuable Player Award.

The MVP was not the only great event of Banks's off-season. One autumn day, he visited a friend's office in downtown Chicago to discuss some business opportunities. The deals the two men discussed have been long forgotten. But on that afternoon, Banks met an attractive young secretary-receptionist named Eloyce Johnson. Johnson, like Banks, was a Texas native; the two hit it off immediately and began dating. At Christmastime, when they were both visiting California—Banks to attend a sports award dinner, Johnson to visit her parents, who had moved to the West Coast—the couple surprised everyone by eloping. Little more than a year later, Eloyce and Ernie Banks became the parents of twin boys, Joey and Jerry—a fitting event for the man who was always saying, "Let's play two!"

# 5

# BASEBALL'S GOLDEN DECADE

*Banks turns the front end of a double play in a 1959 game against the Dodgers as a sliding Junior Gilliam is forced out at second. Though Banks had an average throwing arm, he was smooth and agile at shortstop: in 1959, he posted a record fielding average of .985.*

**M**any baseball historians have chosen the 1950s as the game's most glamorous and colorful decade. Arguably, no other 10-year span in the history of baseball witnessed the heroics of so many truly great players. Willie Mays, Mickey Mantle, Jackie Robinson, Stan Musial, Warren Spahn, Whitey Ford, Henry Aaron, and Ernie Banks were in their prime. Such legends as Joe DiMaggio, Ted Williams, and Bob Feller were winding up their glorious careers. At the same time, future stars such as Al Kaline, Brooks Robinson, Frank Robinson, Eddie Mathews, Sandy Koufax, Bob Gibson, and Don Drysdale were entering the majors.

For the purists among baseball fans, this was indeed the final decade of old-time baseball. There were still only eight teams in each league. The game had not yet witnessed the designated hitter, divisional playoffs, artificial turf, domed stadiums, or large-scale labor disputes. In the 1950s, idealists could still make a case for the view that baseball was a game, not a business.

However, the Chicago Cubs of the 1950s had little to offer that was either glamorous or colorful. Before Ernie Banks came on the scene, the team's major attraction was its historic ballpark. Nestled into a quiet residential neighborhood on Chicago's North Side, Wrigley Field exerted a special charm for fans and players because of its ivy-covered outfield walls and its absence of lights for night baseball. Following World War II, the Cubs were the only team in the major leagues who played all their home games during the daytime. The team's owner, chewing-gum magnate Phil Wrigley, refused to follow the trend toward night games, and loyal Cubs fans usually found a way to get to the ballpark on weekday afternoons.

The Cubs did little to reward their fans' devotion. The team had won three pennants during the 1930s and another in 1945 (though all four trips to the World Series ended in defeat). But in the postwar era, the Cubs were barely competitive, finishing as high as fifth place only once between 1947 and 1957. The club's only gate attraction before the Banks era was Hank Sauer, the strapping outfielder who poled 37 home runs in 1952—that was the year the Cubs finished fifth, and Sauer was named MVP for his role in this accomplishment.

Unfortunately for Cubs fans, Sauer was a one-dimensional player who had only one more good year left. The Cubs obtained slugger Ralph Kiner from the Pirates during the 1953 season, but Kiner was also past his peak and never won a home run crown with the Cubs. For consistent baseball thrills during the 1950s, Chicago's National League fans had to wait until Ernie Banks took over at shortstop. Once he joined the Cubs, he rarely failed to give the faithful what they came to see.

37

Despite his slender build—though standing six feet one, he weighed only 165 pounds as a rookie—Banks proved to be an iron man. When he broke into the Chicago lineup on September 17, 1953, he was there to stay for 424 straight games, setting the all-time record for the most consecutive games played at the beginning of a career. In 1956, an ankle injury finally put Banks in the dugout for 18 days. Then he came right back to establish another streak of 290 games. When another injury forced him to the bench again in 1958, he had played in 714 of 732 ballgames.

With the exception of Dodgers catcher Roy Campanella, none of baseball's leading sluggers had to deal with the day-to-day exertion Banks endured as a middle infielder. Yet none of them put together back-to-back seasons as explosive as the pair Banks enjoyed at the tail end of the decade. Following his MVP performance in 1958, Banks came back with an equally spectacular year in 1959, slugging 45 homers and driving in a league-leading 143 runs. The lofty RBI total was the highest ever recorded by a major league shortstop, and it has never been topped. Banks would also have tied for the N.L. home run crown, but the Braves' Eddie Mathews hit a final circuit blast in a special playoff game and ended the season with 46.

Banks could not single-handedly lead the Cubs to a long-awaited pennant or even make them serious contenders. Yet he did spark the struggling franchise to two straight fifth-place ties, unprecedented success for the post–1945 Cubbies. As a result of this achievement, Banks was fittingly recognized with a second straight MVP Award. Never before had a National League

*Banks slides home in a cloud of dust against the Milwaukee Braves in 1958. In addition to his prowess with the bat and glove, Banks was remarkably durable: despite his slender build, he missed only 18 games during his first five seasons with the Cubs.*

player won the award twice in a row, and only a handful of major leaguers have since duplicated Banks's feat.

Banks might even have been the first ballplayer ever to be MVP three years running. His performance in 1960 was equally solid—he led the league with 41 home runs, and his 117 RBIs were exceeded only by Henry Aaron (126) and Eddie Mathews (124). But the Cubs slipped back to seventh place, a dismal 34 games below

.500. Meanwhile, the surprising Pittsburgh Pirates—the league's worst team during the 1950s—raced to their first pennant in 34 years. The inspired fielding and .325 batting average of Pittsburgh shortstop Dick Groat were crucial to the team's success, and Groat narrowly nipped Banks in the MVP balloting.

For four straight seasons Banks had popped 40 circuit blasts or more. When the statistics were tallied at the end of baseball's golden decade, no other slugger could match the output of the Chicago shortstop. In the six seasons that stretched from 1955 to 1960, Banks had swatted 248 homers; behind him stood Mantle with 236, Mathews with 226, Mays with 214, and Aaron with 206. For the same period Banks was the RBI leader as well with 694, outpacing Aaron at 674, Mathews at 605, Mays at 601, and Mantle at 589.

As the decade came to an end, the Cubs management realized that the franchise could not enter the 1960s relying on Banks to provide the team's only point of interest. Unable to surround their star shortstop with an able supporting cast, Phil Wrigley and his advisers launched an experiment that would become one of the most bizarre affairs in the annals of baseball: they fired manager Lou Boudreau and decided not to hire a replacement.

As it turned out, the Cubs did not exactly play baseball without a manager. Instead, they played the 1961 and 1962 seasons with a whole committee of managers. The idea was called a "college of coaches": coaches Elvin Tappe, Lou Klein, Vedie Himsl, and Harry Craft took turns making on-field decisions. The front office reasoned that four managerial brains would clearly

*Selling cars in a Chicago dealership, Banks touts the virtues of a new model in November 1959. On the verge of winning his second straight MVP Award, Banks was Chicago's number one sports hero; but like every other player of that era, he still needed to get a job in the off-season.*

be better than one. What was missing, unfortunately, was any clear-cut authority and any obvious direction for the hapless team.

Needless to say, Chicago's college of coaches did not start a trend in baseball strategy. While the scheme was in effect, the Cubs finished seventh and then ninth (in a newly expanded 10-team league). Indeed, the 1962 season was one of the all-time lows in Cubs history, as the team finished with a record of 59-103, 42 games out of first place; only the brand-new New York

Mets, who lost a record 120 games and finished 60 games out, suffered through a more dismal season. The Chicago front office finally gave up the odd experiment and hired Bob Kennedy to manage the team for the 1963 season, when the Cubs rebounded to 82-80, their best record in 17 years.

One positive result of the strange managerial experiment did emerge in early 1961. Slowed by an ankle injury in spring training, Banks had lost a step at shortstop and was again having difficulty reaching balls hit to his left and right. The college of coaches tried him out in left field, but Banks could not adjust to the outfield. Finally, Elvin Tappe took Banks out for breakfast and asked him how he felt about shifting to first base. Banks, always a diplomat and a team player, had no complaints about the Cubs' strange managerial system or about the request for a mid-career shift in position. "I told Tappe that I would do anything to help the Cubs," he recalled. "Had he asked me to catch I would have done it."

Unlike the failed experiment at third base in 1957, the move to first turned out to be permanent. After 1,125 games at shortstop, Banks went on to play 1,259 more at first base. "There can be no question that my move to first base has prolonged my career," he said shortly afterward, "and I've been happy playing there. It's not a bad place to call my own."

# 6

# THE SEASON THAT MIGHT HAVE BEEN

*Banks watches one of his round-trippers leave the ballpark during the 1969 season. After playing for mediocre teams for 15 years, Banks was finally able to dream of a National League pennant, as the Cubs were widely favored to win their division.*

**M**ost longtime big league stars can reflect back on a single great career season—the year when everything seemed to fall perfectly into place for both him and his teammates. In such a dream season, the team finishes in first place, postseason heroics follow, and ideally baseball's highest goal—a World Series ring—is finally achieved. A few lucky players may even experience several such seasons before their career has come to its final summer. For the majority, one great moment in the spotlight is the most that might be dreamed of.

For Ernie Banks, Chicago's greatest baseball hero, there was never to be such a season. The Cubs teams for which Banks played throughout his two baseball decades were almost always dreadful. Year in and year out, Banks was their only all-star, their only true asset. During the 1950s, no Cubs pitcher ever won 20 games in a season; with the exception of Hank Sauer, who was traded only a year after Banks arrived, no Cubs hitter apart from Banks led the league in any major offensive category. No matter how hard Banks pounded the ball, there was no way he could single-handedly lead the Cubs to a pennant or even into the first division.

During the 1960s, as Elvis Presley, drive-in movies, and Hula Hoops gave way to the Beatles, antiwar protests, and the civil rights movement, the baseball outlook on the North Side of Chicago slowly improved. Though the team continued to wallow at the bottom of the standings, the front office was finally able to sign and develop some talented young players. Ron Santo, a hard-hitting and sure-handed third baseman, became a regular in 1961, as did outfielder Billy Williams, who eventually posted a .297 lifetime batting average. Shortstop Don Kessinger and second baseman Glenn Beckert arrived in 1965, giving the Cubs a first-rate middle infield. Randy Hundley, a solid defensive catcher and a clever handler of pitchers, came over in a trade from the Giants in 1966.

Even more important, there was some real pitching for Hundley to work with. Ken Holtzman, a hard-throwing left-hander, joined the rotation in 1966. During the same year, the Chicagoans made a brilliant trade with the Philadelphia Phillies, obtaining a tall right-hander from Ontario, Canada—Ferguson Jenkins. Jenkins would turn out to be the finest Cubs hurler since the legendary Mordecai "Three Finger" Brown, who had pitched his last game for the team back in 1912. Like Brown, Jenkins was to post six consecutive 20-win seasons in a Chicago uniform; together with Holtzman, he gave the Cubs world-class pitching to complement their improved hitting and defense.

At first, the Cubs seemed to go backward in spite of their improving talent. Eighth-place finishes in 1964 and 1965 cost Bob Kennedy his managerial job. The Cubs then hired Leo "the Lip" Durocher, a hard-nosed veteran who had

successfully piloted both the New York Giants and the Brooklyn Dodgers. Durocher knew his baseball, but during his first season at the helm the Cubs hit rock bottom with a 59-103 record, sinking below even the lowly New York Mets. Banks himself had a lackluster year, hitting only 15 home runs and driving in 75 runs.

During the following year, the Cubs' new players began to jell. With Ron Santo belting 31 home runs, Banks contributing 23, and Jenkins posting his first 20-win season, the Cubs scored a league-high 702 runs and shot up to third place, 13 games over .500. Exactly 20 years had passed since the Cubs had been in the first division at season's end. When the team finished third again in 1968, they made it clear that they were a force to be reckoned with.

As the teams went to spring training in 1969, the Cubs found themselves in an unusual position. Due to the addition of two more expansion teams, the National League had been split into eastern and western divisions, each consisting of six teams. Four of the league's best teams, the San Francisco Giants, the Cincinnati Reds, the Atlanta Braves, and the Los Angeles Dodgers, were now in the West. Of the teams remaining in

*Hall of Famer Billy Williams hit 376 home runs and batted .297 during his 15 seasons with the Cubs. With sluggers such as Williams, Banks, and Ron Santo in their lineup, the Cubs were always dangerous—but they did not become contenders until they improved their pitching in the late 1960s.*

the N.L. East, the Cubs and the defending champion St. Louis Cardinals were clearly the best. Most of the baseball pundits felt that the Cards were fading and the Cubs were peaking: they predicted that Chicago would breeze to the division crown in 1969.

The Cubs now had the burden of making these predictions come true. At the outset, events appeared to conspire against them. During the winter, the major league owners and the players' union wrangled over a new pension plan for the players. Spring training was delayed while the dispute dragged on, and for a while the entire season appeared to be in jeopardy. When the teams finally reported for spring training, it almost looked as if the Cubs might have been better off staying away.

The pitchers had lost valuable time in getting their arms into shape, and as a result the team dropped eight of its first nine exhibition games. But for some reason a victory over the Seattle Pilots, an American League expansion team, turned things around. A new spirit took hold of the Cubs as they won 11 of their final 17 preseason outings.

Regular-season play saw the Cubbies continue their sudden hot streak with a vengeance. On opening day, a pinch two-run homer by reserve outfielder Willie Smith sparked a dramatic 7–6 victory over Philadelphia. The Cubs were at home for the season's first full week and took advantage by chalking up seven victories in eight starts. And soon the Cubbies were thrilling their long-suffering fans by taking a firm grip on first place. For 156 days, they stood at the top of the standings, while attendance at Wrigley Field soared toward a new record of nearly 1.7 million.

The season was filled with individual highlights. In April, Billy Williams smacked four doubles in a single game to tie a long-standing major league mark. Banks drove home seven runs on May 13, during a 19–0 rout of the San Diego Padres. In June, Don Kessinger established a new major league record with 54 straight error-less games at shortstop. And on August 19, Ken Holtzman pitched a masterful no-hit game against the Braves.

For Banks, one of the year's brightest moments occurred off the field, miles from Chicago. The 1969 All-Star Game was being held in Washington, D.C., and the festivities included a black-tie dinner celebrating the 100th anniversary of major league baseball. At the dinner, hosted by baseball commissioner Bowie Kuhn, Banks learned that the Chicago fans had voted him the greatest Cubs player of all time. If that were not enough, a panel of experts had chosen Banks as the third leading shortstop of baseball's first 100 years—only the incomparable Honus Wagner and Boston Red Sox great Joe Cronin were deemed superior.

As the second half of the season got under way, it soon became apparent to baseball fans that the Cubs were not the only news story in the National League. The New York Mets, a running joke since their debut in 1962, were suddenly in second place, and they were acting like genuine contenders. Position by position, the Mets could not compare with the Cubs. Chicago's lineup was loaded with all-stars, while the Mets fielded a blend of unheralded young-sters and fading veterans. But the New Yorkers had the best pitching in the league, as the Cubs had begun to realize on July 9 when Tom Seaver just missed throwing a perfect game against them. With tight fielding behind their pitchers and a heads-up, mistake-free style of play instilled by manager Gil Hodges, the Mets gave nothing away. They made up for their lack of punch with timely hitting, and as the season went on they began to believe that they were a team of destiny.

In mid-August, the Cubs still enjoyed a comfortable 9½-game lead. But at the beginning of September, the Mets made their fateful run at the title. And the Cubs helped them out by diving into a hopeless tailspin. A summer of celebration quickly became a tragic finale for Chicago. The New Yorkers won 22 of their final 27 contests, as Seaver won his final 10 starts in a row and Jerry Koosman his last 9. On September 10, the Mets took over first place and went on to win the division by 8 games. The Cubs had helped them out by not even managing to play .500 baseball during the second half of the season.

In the soul-searching that followed, many reasons were offered for the Cubs' horrible collapse. Perhaps the most popular theory contended that playing all their home games in daylight hours during the hottest stretches of July and August had sapped the energy of the Chicago players. Another theory speculated that the Cubs players let success go to their heads by midseason and devoted too much time to personal activities such as commercials and public appearances.

In addition, many fans and sportswriters complained that Leo Durocher had misused his pitchers, never rested his older regulars down the stretch, and maintained too tense an atmosphere in the Cubs clubhouse. Few critics were willing to concede the obvious: the New York Mets had simply been the better team in 1969, almost unbeatable in September and determined not to let anyone deny them their first-ever world championship. Their postseason victories over the heavily favored Braves and Orioles proved the point.

*Cubs outfielder Jim Hickman congratulates Banks on a second-inning home run against the Houston Astros on August 24, 1969. At the time, the Cubs were still leading the N.L. East; but on September 10, the New York Mets overtook them and went on to win the division.*

As always, Banks came through the disheartening experience of the late-season foldup with the same cheerful and optimistic nature that marked his entire baseball life. Banks had certainly done his own part to spur the Cubs on to a long-awaited pennant. At age 38 he had remained the backbone of the offense, driving home 106 runs. He had, in fact, set a new big league record for a player of his age, surpassing the standard of 103 RBIs established by the 38-year-old Babe Ruth all the way back in 1933. No one in the city of Chicago could have been more pained than the 15-year veteran, who had played on so many lackluster ballclubs and longed so fiercely to play in a World Series. But when the dreamed-of pennant was snatched away from him, Banks was philosophical. "It was just not meant to be," he reflected wistfully. And then in the next breath he added, "But things will be heavenly in nineteen-seventy!"

As it turned out, 1970 was little more than a last great hurrah for Banks and his Cubs teammates. With Billy Williams carrying the offense, the team was in the pennant race, but they had not recovered from the collapse of the previous year—deep down, the Cubs did not believe they could win. In the end, they did achieve a small measure of revenge by beating out the Mets for second place.

Banks was clearly coming to the end of the road. Troubled by aching knees, he played in only 72 games and came to the plate a mere 222 times, a steep decline for a player who had chalked up more than 500 at-bats 12 times during his career and more than 600 at-bats 3 times. Even in his limited playing time, Banks showed that he could still do damage, accounting for 12 home runs and 44 RBIs. But his days as a perennial N.L. all-star were over. Only a handful of personal milestones remained for the 39-year-old warrior.

Banks had entered the 1970 campaign in close pursuit of his 500th career homer, a total that had been achieved up to then by only eight other players in baseball history: Babe Ruth, Jimmie Foxx, Mel Ott, Ted Williams, Henry Aaron, Willie Mays, Mickey Mantle, and Eddie

*Despite his bitter disappointment in 1969, the ever-optimistic Banks declared, "Things will be heavenly in nineteenseventy!" But the Cubs finished second again, and Banks's aching knees made him only a part-time player.*

Mathews. On May 12, 1970, Banks finally joined that illustrious club, although with something less than the ceremony and hoopla that might have been expected for such a landmark event.

On the morning of May 12, heavy rain pelted the Chicago area. The weather cleared up by game time, but only 5,624 hardy fans had made their way to Wrigley Field. They were rewarded for their loyalty when Banks slammed an inside pitch from Atlanta's Pat Jarvis into the screen behind the left-field bleachers. The sparse crowd let loose with a noisy celebration as their hero rounded the basepaths. The cheering continued long after Banks returned to the dugout; it did not subside until he had come out for three separate curtain calls, tipping his cap and bowing to his adoring public.

Banks was even more jovial than usual when reporters mobbed him in the clubhouse. "Do you know this is Tuesday and every Tuesday is Senior Citizen's Day at Wrigley Field?" he chimed up. "Old Ern did this for his own special people!"

Even though the clock was winding down on his career, Banks remained a vital force in Chicago's baseball life. Whenever he sat out a game, he would make an appearance in the broadcast booth as a guest commentator, sharing his enthusiasm for the game with fans throughout the Chicago area. His teammates found him consistently inspiring. "All he wants to do is play baseball," Fergie Jenkins remarked. "And when he isn't playing baseball, he wants to talk baseball." Ron Santo explained the appeal of Banks's personality to fans and teammates. "He cares about other things," Santo observed. "He cares about life. He cares about people. In the nine or ten years I've known him, he's never changed a bit. Home runs or strikeouts, nothing ever gets him down. When he was going poorly it affected him inside, maybe, but he was still smiling and chattering and saying happy things to people and encouraging people."

Despite his aching knees, Banks was able to reach a few more milestones in late 1970 and early in the 1971 season. His final home run, the 512th, tied him with longtime rival Eddie Mathews for seventh on the all-time list. He also passed the 4,700 mark in total bases, placing him in the top 15 in baseball history. But by midseason 1971, after playing in only 39 games and batting a mere .193, Banks finally decided to hang up his spikes.

Banks clearly missed the joy of competition, but on the surface, he remained as cheerful and optimistic as ever. He continued to be a familiar figure at Wrigley Field while he served the ballclub as director of community relations. His stature in Chicago was higher than ever. In 1969 and 1970 he had been voted Chicagoan of the Year, and he served on the boards of numerous organizations, including Jackson Park Hospital, the Glenwood Home for Boys, the Chicago Rehabilitation Institute, and Big Brothers. He was so popular that an alderman proposed erecting a statue of him in the center of Chicago.

Having been one of the game's earliest black superstars, Banks had entertained the idea of becoming baseball's first black manager. "I've tried to picture myself as a manager," he once admitted. "Sometimes I like the idea." But he did not pursue this goal aggressively; when the subject came up, he preferred to talk about other men he judged as perhaps more deserving of the honor: "At the superstar level four men definitely merit managerial consideration: Hank

*Banks crosses home plate after clouting his 507th lifetime home run on June 30, 1970, against the Cardinals in St. Louis. During the previous month, he had become only the ninth player in baseball history to reach the 500–home run mark.*

Aaron, Willie Mays, Maury Wills, and Frank Robinson. All these men have made contributions above and beyond their playing ability. They have earned respect and demonstrated the importance of good leadership. This is what baseball is all about, and it is the reason I consider all my teammates and my fellow major leaguers as brothers." Banks was deeply gratified when, in 1975, the Cleveland Indians made baseball history by naming Frank Robinson as their manager.

When it came to the Hall of Fame, only Banks himself had any doubt about his election. "To me a superstar is a person with ability beyond all reason," he had observed near the end of his career, "and I never have seen myself that way. All I've done has just sort of come to me. I never dreamed of being any sort of star. The Hall of Fame? Are you kidding me? I've had reward enough just lasting in the big leagues this long!" When Banks became eligible for Cooperstown in 1976, the nation's baseball writers had no doubts about his place among the game's immortals. They gave him the added distinction of being only the eighth player elected to the Hall in his very first year of eligiblity.

More than two decades after his last game, Banks remained the foremost symbol of Cubs baseball. Even the new generation of fans who never saw him play still identified Banks as Mr. Cub and listened eagerly as older fans recalled his feats at Wrigley Field in the days before the old ballpark had lights. When the club finally bowed to pressure and installed lights, the lords of baseball responded by staging the 1990 All-Star Game at Wrigley. No one in the capacity crowd was surprised to see Ernie Banks in the spotlight during the pregame ceremonies.

Invited to throw out the ceremonial first ball, Banks was perfectly in character. He went to the mound with his young granddaughter and introduced her to the crowd as a baseball star of the future. Then he helped the delighted youngster get off a throw to home plate. Rather than simply basking in the adoration of the hometown fans, Banks chose to make a point about the importance of family and the desire of female athletes for greater opportunity and recognition.

Banks's charisma was not lost on the nation's advertising industry: in 1993, he was recruited for a series of American Express com-

*A few pounds over his playing weight but still trim and dapper, the 62-year-old Banks throws out the first ball at the Cubs home opener in April 1993. A successful executive and a director of many Chicago charities, Banks remains the all-time favorite at Wrigley Field.*

mercials featuring Hall of Fame ballplayers. In the ads, each of the retired greats—Banks, Henry Aaron, Stan Musial, Brooks Robinson, and Al Kaline—spoke movingly about the joys of baseball and the thrill of being in Cooperstown. Banks's spot was unique because he once again made a vivid statement about equal opportunity. "I found out I had quick hands when I was picking cotton," he said with a grin, reminding viewers that when he was a youth black ballplayers were excluded from the majors. In this context, he went on to express his love of the game and his happiness about being enshrined at Cooperstown.

Of all the many baseball people who have been exposed to Banks's magnetic personality, perhaps Frank "Trader" Lane, the onetime general manager of the Chicago White Sox, best summed up the great shortstop's appeal. "Banks is a hundred billboards on a hundred highways," Lane declared. "He's baseball's best advertisement. And he's priceless!"

In today's baseball world, where superstars are measured by their salaries as much as by their batting averages, there might not have been a contract large enough to reward the man who remains the foremost living symbol of all that is best about the game of baseball.

# CHRONOLOGY

| | |
|---|---|
| 1931 | Born Ernest Banks in Dallas, Texas, on January 31 |
| 1948 | While starring in football and basketball at Washington High School, joins Detroit Colts baseball team for summer barnstorming tour |
| 1950 | Graduates from high school; signs professional baseball contract with Kansas City Monarchs of the Negro American League; tours with Jackie Robinson's all-star team |
| 1951–52 | Serves with U.S. Army in Germany, playing on army baseball team |
| 1953 | Returns to Monarchs, who sell his contract to the Chicago Cubs; makes his major league debut on September 17; hits first major league home run on September 20 |
| 1954 | Finishes first full season in majors with 19 home runs and 79 RBIs |
| 1955 | Hits record five grand slams; establishes his credentials as a slugger with 44 home runs and 117 RBIs |
| 1956 | Sets record for most consecutive games played (424) at the start of a major league career |
| 1958 | Hits 47 home runs, highest total ever for a major league shortstop; wins MVP Award; marries Eloyce Johnson |
| 1959 | Finishes season with fewest errors (12) and highest fielding percentage (.985) ever recorded by a major league shortstop; becomes first N.L. player in history to win MVP Award two years in a row |
| 1960 | Finishes season with 41 home runs, leading the major leagues for the second time; twin sons, Joey and Jerry, are born |
| 1961 | Banks moves from shortstop to first base, where he remains for the rest of his career |
| 1962 | Hits 300th career home run |
| 1969 | Selected by Chicago fans as greatest Cubs player of all time |
| 1970 | Hits 500th career home run in Wrigley Field |
| 1971 | Retires after 19 seasons and becomes Cubs director of community relations |
| 1977 | Inducted into the Baseball Hall of Fame, after becoming only the eighth player selected in his first year of eligibility |

ERNEST BANKS
"MR. CUB"
CHICAGO N. L., 1953-1971
HIT 512 CAREER HOMERS WITH MORE THAN
40 IN A SEASON FIVE TIMES. HAD RECORD
FIVE GRAND-SLAMS IN 1955. FIRST TO BE
ELECTED N. L. MOST VALUABLE PLAYER TWO
SUCCESSIVE YEARS, 1958-59. LED LEAGUE
IN HOME RUNS AND RUNS BATTED IN TWICE
AND SLUGGING PCT. ONCE. ESTABLISHED
RECORDS FOR MOST HOMERS IN SEASON BY
SHORTSTOP (47 IN 1958) AND FOR FEWEST
ERRORS (12) AND BEST FIELDING AVERAGE
(.985) BY A SHORTSTOP IN 1959.

# MAJOR LEAGUE STATISTICS

## CHICAGO CUBS

| YEAR | TEAM | G | AB | R | H | 2B | 3B | HR | RBI | BA | SB |
|------|------|------|------|------|------|------|------|------|------|------|------|
| 1953 | CHI N | 10 | 35 | 3 | 11 | 1 | 1 | 2 | 6 | .314 | 0 |
| 1954 | | 154 | 593 | 70 | 163 | 19 | 7 | 19 | 79 | .275 | 6 |
| 1955 | | 154 | 596 | 98 | 176 | 29 | 9 | 44 | 117 | .295 | 9 |
| 1956 | | 139 | 538 | 82 | 160 | 25 | 8 | 28 | 85 | .297 | 6 |
| 1957 | | 156 | 594 | 113 | 169 | 34 | 6 | 43 | 102 | .285 | 8 |
| 1958 | | 154 | 617 | 119 | 193 | 23 | 11 | 47 | 129 | .313 | 4 |
| 1959 | | 155 | 589 | 97 | 179 | 25 | 6 | 45 | 143 | .304 | 2 |
| 1960 | | 156 | 597 | 94 | 162 | 32 | 7 | 41 | 117 | .271 | 1 |
| 1961 | | 138 | 511 | 75 | 142 | 22 | 4 | 29 | 80 | .278 | 1 |
| 1962 | | 154 | 610 | 87 | 164 | 20 | 6 | 37 | 104 | .269 | 5 |
| 1963 | | 130 | 432 | 41 | 98 | 20 | 1 | 18 | 64 | .227 | 0 |
| 1964 | | 157 | 591 | 67 | 156 | 29 | 6 | 23 | 95 | .264 | 1 |
| 1965 | | 163 | 612 | 79 | 162 | 25 | 3 | 28 | 106 | .265 | 3 |
| 1966 | | 141 | 511 | 52 | 139 | 23 | 7 | 15 | 75 | .272 | 0 |
| 1967 | | 151 | 573 | 68 | 158 | 26 | 4 | 23 | 95 | .276 | 2 |
| 1968 | | 150 | 552 | 71 | 136 | 27 | 0 | 32 | 83 | .246 | 2 |
| 1969 | | 155 | 565 | 60 | 143 | 19 | 2 | 23 | 106 | .253 | 0 |
| 1970 | | 72 | 222 | 25 | 56 | 6 | 2 | 12 | 44 | .252 | 0 |
| 1971 | | 39 | 83 | 4 | 16 | 2 | 0 | 3 | 6 | .193 | 0 |
| **Totals** | | 2528 | 9421 | 1305 | 2583 | 407 | 90 | 512 | 1636 | .274 | 50 |

**All-Star Games**

| | | | | | | | | | | | |
|------|------|------|------|------|------|------|------|------|------|------|------|
| 10 years | | 13 | 33 | 4 | 10 | 3 | 1 | 1 | 3 | .303 | 0 |

# FURTHER READING

Banks, Ernie, and Jim Enright. *Mr. Cub.* Chicago: Follett, 1971.

Daley, Arthur. "Ernie Banks." In *All the Home Run Kings.* New York: Putnam, 1972.

Furlong, William B. "Ernie Banks' Life with a Loser." *Sport*, April 1963.

———. "Ernie Banks." In *The Third Fireside Book of Baseball*, Charles Einstein, ed. New York: Simon & Schuster, 1968.

Gifford, Barry. The *Neighborhood of Baseball: A Personal History of the Chicago Cubs.* New York: Dutton, 1981.

Langford, Jim. *The Game is Never Over: An Appreciative History of the Chicago Cubs, 1948–1980.* South Bend, IN: Icarus Press, 1980.

———. *Runs, Hits and Errors: A Treasury of Cub History and Humor.* South Bend, IN: Diamond Communications, 1987.

Libby, Bill. "Why They Call Ernie Banks 'Baseball's Beautiful Man'." *Sport*, June 1969.

———. *Ernie Banks: Mr. Cub.* New York: Putnam, 1971.

May, Julian. *Ernie Banks, Home Run Slugger.* Mankato, MN: Crestwood House, 1973.

Reidenbaugh, Lowell. *Cooperstown: Where Baseball's Legends Live Forever.* St. Louis: The Sporting News Publishing Company, 1983.

Shapiro, Milton J. "Ernie Banks." In *Champions of the Bat.* New York: Julian Messner, 1968.

Talley, Rick. *The Cubs of '69: Recollections of the Team That Should Have Been.* Chicago: Contemporary Books, 1989.

# INDEX

---

PICTURE CREDITS
AP/Wide World Photos: pp. 2, 11, 31, 45, 46, 50, 54, 56; History and Archives Division, Dallas Public Library: p. 12; The *Kansas City Call*: p. 18; Brooks Lawrence Collection: p. 24; National Baseball Library, Cooperstown, NY: pp. 21, 60; The *Sporting News*: pp. 42, 58; UPI/Bettmann: pp. 8, 15, 26, 28, 34, 38, 40, 49.

PETER C. BJARKMAN, also known as "Doctor Baseball," is the author of more than 20 baseball biographies and history books, including the two-volume *Encyclopedia of Major League Baseball Team Histories*, *The Baseball Scrapbook*, and *Baseball & the Game of Life: Stories for the Thinking Fan*. In addition, he has written *The History of the NBA* and the *Encyclopedia of Pro Basketball Team Histories*. Dr. Bjarkman has also taught English and linguistics at Purdue University and the University of Colorado and currently lives in Lafayette, Indiana, with his wife, Dr. Ronnie Wilbur, a college professor. He is also the author of *Roberto Clemente*, *Duke Snider*, and *Warren Spahn* in the Chelsea House BASEBALL LEGENDS series.

JIM MURRAY, veteran sports columnist of the *Los Angeles Times*, is one of America's most acclaimed writers. He has been named "America's Best Sportswriter" by the National Association of Sportscasters and Sportswriters 14 times, was awarded the Red Smith Award, and was twice winner of the National Headliner Award. In addition, he was awarded the J. G. Taylor Spink Award in 1987 for "meritorious contributions to baseball writing." With this award came his 1988 induction into the National Baseball Hall of Fame in Cooperstown, New York. In 1990, Jim Murray was awarded the Pulitzer Prize for Commentary.

EARL WEAVER is the winningest manager in the Baltimore Orioles' history by a wide margin. He compiled 1,480 victories in his 17 years at the helm. After managing eight different minor league teams, he was given the chance to lead the Orioles in 1968. Under his leadership the Orioles finished lower than second place in the American League East only four times in 17 years. One of only 12 managers in big league history to have managed in four or more World Series, Earl was named Manager of the Year in 1979. The popular Weaver had his number 5 retired in 1982, joining Brooks Robinson, Frank Robinson, and Jim Palmer, whose numbers were retired previously. Earl Weaver continues his association with the professional baseball scene by writing, broadcasting, and coaching.